FREESTYLE

DANCE

BY

ANNA JONES

ISBN: 0 900326 30 1

DEDICATED TO MY PARENTS

HENRY & MAIR GOODALL

Printed and published by
International Dance Publications ©
International House
76 Bennett Road, Brighton BN2 5JL

First Print July 1995
Reprinted May 1996
Revised February 2000
Reprinted May 2002
Revised May 2004
Reprinted May 2006

ANNA JONES

Past President of the International Dance Teachers' Association.
International adjudicator, coach and lecturer.
Fellow and Examiner IDTA.
Co-trainer of reigning United Kingdom, British,
International and Universal Freestyle Champions.
Former Latin-American Champion.
Carl-Alan Award Winner
Millennium Lifetime Achievement Award Winner
Le Classique de Danse Award Winner.
Fellow of the Institute of Medical Laboratory Sciences.

CONTENTS

$^{\$}$ Lycra is a Registered Trade Mark of Dupont

FOREWORD

I am delighted with the publication of this book. It is the product of dance teachers dedicated to this modern style who recognised in it great possibilities for enjoyment and achievement.

Understandably the boom generated by the film "Saturday Night Fever" attracted opportunists and as the dance form developed beyond the social level it embraced athleticism even acrobatics. The ballroom dancing profession viewed with trepidation the limited competence and lack of essential knowledge of many who taught the style. It was clear that special training and an appropriate examination structure had to be instituted.

At that time I was chairman of the British Council of Ballroom Dancing and from 1983 until 1989, when I retired, I was chairman or co-chairman of numerous committees that produced a technique for professional examinations and a structure for amateur competitions. On the committees sat representatives of all recognised ballroom dancing associations - members of the British Council of Ballroom Dancing and the Association of Disco and Freestyle Professionals, an organisation of teachers with a special interest in Freestyle dancing.

The committee work continued and has now produced a syllabus for elementary, intermediate and advanced professional examinations. All and more on advanced dancing is included in this publication.

My delight in the publication of this book lies not only in the fact that a common syllabus has been created but in the unity of purpose that produced it.

Anna Jones is to be congratulated on the leadership and industry she has shown in putting the book together. Anna's qualifications are impressive - highly qualified in several dance styles. She is a championship performer and coach and is much in demand for lectures at home and overseas. In another respect Anna is exceptional - she holds a Post Graduate Diploma in Medical Microbiology.

LEONARD MORGAN

PREFACE

It had always been my intention to write a book on Freestyle Dance and I had planned to do this much earlier in its development. However, by leaving it until now has meant that I have been able to include a little more "history" and a greater number of steps & movements that have developed over recent years.

With a comprehensive examination structure from Student through to Fellowship in place, it is, of course essential that the technique be at its best, in order to "stand up tall" next to the other dance forms. I have endeavoured to aim for the "middle-ground" which stays within the realms of dance related information.

It is very important for teachers of this form of dance to understand the basic workings of the human body so that they are fully aware of movements that can cause harm to a dancer.

In the early days of Freestyle, I was Chairman of the ADFP Technical Committee following for 5 years as the joint Chairman of the BCBD\ADFP Technical & Rules Committee with Leonard Morgan until my resignation in 1992. During this time, I had the pleasure of working with professionals who also had great enthusiasm for the development of a Freestyle technique. Their input ultimately helped to create the joint technique of the BCBD/ADFP. I would therefore like to acknowledge Audrey Andrews, Lilian Aubrey, Tony Bill, Diane Corbett, Margaret Cox, Barry Davids, Frances Dawson, Rosemary Oakes, Jean Rowbotham and Peggy Spencer MBE; plus fellow professionals I have since worked with on the IDTA Freestyle Committee - Frances Clayton, Kenneth Lee, Bill Phillips, Jack Rayner, Jacqueline Roberts, Ros Wicks and Phil Winston.

There are numerous Freestyle teachers throughout the country who work hard on the technique committees of all the other dance associations and those who continue to improve the standard of Freestyle through their dedication within their own schools and/or by lecturing throughout the country.

I would like to acknowledge the contribution that has been made to Freestyle by David Jones who has been responsible for introducing so many of the ideas that are used by most of today's top competitors. Much of this work is now so well established that it is sometimes difficult to remember from whence it came.

I hope that this book will be useful in one way or another to all Freestyle teachers. I plan to revise the book regularly in order that new movements and developments can be included and work that becomes naturally extinct can be removed. In this way my book should help as an up to date reference on Freestyle Dance.

It is very important to remember that those using the book as an aid to professional qualifications must check the most up to date syllabus of their Association/Society to ensure which items they are required to know for the particular degree they are taking.

My gratitude to Diana Poole who typed the manuscript.

A BRIEF HISTORY OF FREESTYLE DANCE

Since the decline of the "Teddy Boy" era in the late 1950's there had been no major new dance craze to follow Rock & Roll. During the 60's and 70's there had always been what was commonly termed "beat dancing". As the name implies, this simply refers to any type of dance, excluding recognised forms, that was performed to the beat played by pop groups of the day. For many years it involved stepping from one foot or the other with slight movement of the hips and arms, according to whatever idea was in fashion in a particular town or area. This type of dancing was occasionally interspersed with a craze that involved one or two specific movements and had a particular name, e.g. *Twist, Locomotion* and *March of the Mods.*

In 1978 the era of Disco dancing was truly born in the UK. For months we had waited with baited breath whilst Americans went wild under the spell of the dance craze sweeping the USA and all this was due to one film and primarily one performer, John Travolta in *Saturday Night Fever.* Travolta was able to bring the message across to millions of young people that here was a lad of working class background with a mundane 9 till 5 poorly paid job, who was able to become successful in a different way - he could dance, and dance well. His reputation at the local Discotheque became a legend and when he entered this atmosphere at night he was respected and hero-worshipped by one and all.

In the film Travolta had a couple of solo spots when he showed off his rhythmic talents, his hip gyrations (causing quite a stir) and acrobatic movements leaving onlookers aghast! In hindsight, the movements now appear so tame and some of the sequences have dubious phrasing. However, the film must be recognised as a unique type of musical which brought a new dance form to this country.

The public yearned to know how to perform the very steps that Travolta had danced in the film and, to begin with, it was difficult to piece the routines together as they did not appear as complete sequences in the film. The release of the film came shortly before the true age of the video and very few people had a video recorder of any description in their own home. It was, therefore, necessary to literally sit through the film many times just to see the dance routines enough times to piece them together with, of course, the aid of quick note taking and a photographic memory! Some professionals managed to pick up the routines in this way and then pass on the information as soon as possible after the film's London debut.

At the same time, Antony Allen from Brighton made several trips to the States in order to bring back much of the Disco work emanating from *Saturday Night Fever* and the numerous line dances which followed in the wake of the film.. As well as Disco, he brought back many Hustle variations - Hustle being a style of dance also made popular by the film.

Dance classes specialising in the 'Night Fever' routines boomed in all areas of the country and many teachers were obviously delighted with this sudden surge in business. With the re-release of the film as an 'A' version after its original 'X' production, a new cinema audience of thousands of younger people emerged and hence expanded the classes even further.

What this film had done was to bring young people back into the dance schools after a relative decline of many years. It had suddenly become the norm for young lads, as well as girls, to take up dancing as a hobby and attend classes or take private lessons. Ultimately, the film had created Utopia for the younger generation - they could learn the sort of dancing that appealed to them the most and perform it to their own type of music, that which most of them chose to listen to every day.

After the public had learnt all the routines included in the film, plenty abandoned the classes as many schools did not continue along the theme that had been set. It was at this point that a number of professionals decided to continue where the film had left off. Using the best of the records available in the charts at the time, they began working out routines for their own classes, tentatively at first, increasing in confidence as the classes soared and their pupils continued to enjoy the work they were doing.

As time progressed, more varied and interesting work was included, graded according to the standard of the class, ultimately using greater rhythmical interpretation and use of more parts of the body.

Teachers workshops were organised in several parts of the country initially by Peggy Spencer MBE, Patricia Thompson, Michael Stylianos and Anne Lingard. These were designed for teachers to gain ideas from fellow professionals and created a stimulus for class and medal work.

Medal tests for Disco/Freestyle have been very popular since they were first introduced. In fact, as early as 1981, one Dance Association had already announced that the number of medal tests taken in Disco during the year had exceeded the joint number taken in Ballroom, Latin-American, and Old Time Dancing. The syllabus for Disco/Freestyle medal tests has largely been left to the discretion of individual teachers; they are thus able to create a medal test structure increasing in complexity towards the higher awards in relation to the standard and type of work taught at a particular school.

National Disco/Freestyle competitions, specifically aimed at the medallist pupil, are regularly staged in the UK by most Associations and these provide a good introduction to competitive work in an atmosphere free from most of the Championship class competitors, where the overall achievement of each dance school represented is usually taken into account at the end of the day. These competitions provide a good platform from which competitors can move on into the field of Open Championship competitions if desired.

The first major Dance Championship of its kind was held at the Cat's Whiskers Ballroom in Streatham London, on August Bank Holiday 1978. The Organiser was Bobby Short and the sole Adjudicator for the day was Sue Manachek of 'Legs & Co.', who must have been presented with an awesome task, as nobody could have predicted just how big this inaugural event was going to be! Those who attended realised that we were on the threshold of something very big. The sheer numbers and the utter enthusiasm that prevailed throughout the ballroom heralded the start of this era of competitive Disco/Freestyle dancing which has grown with each passing year. After the first big competition at the Cat's Whiskers, several more were immediately organised and during the following twelve months, about six major events were staged, mostly by John and Arlene Leach, who also ran the first Disco Festival. Since then, many more competitions have been organised and most major titles are staged annually by the prominent promoters.

The Association of Dance and Freestyle Professionals (ADFP) was established soon after the advent of the competition scene as there was no controlling body taking an interest in the competitive aspect of this type of dance. Professionals from all of the dance associations thus got together and gradually formulated a tiered grading and age group structure, as well as organising lecture days for the teachers and national team matches for the dancers etc. The ADFP joined with the British Dance Council (BCD) to become the joint controlling body of all Disco/Freestyle competitions throughout the UK and are responsible for rule changes and granting of championships. Together they produced a combined Technique of Disco/Freestyle Dancing, which was used by most dance associations for the training and qualifying of teachers in this field.

The term Freestyle has largely replaced Disco over recent years and this is mainly due to the directions that the dance form has taken during this time. Disco, obviously related to the type of steps and movements that were, and still are, performed in a Discotheque. They are basically quite simple, can easily be performed and require very little space. Progress has seen a marked development of many basic movements including runs, kicks, spins and the like, none of which could be performed easily in a Discotheque. Most of the class work used in schools now involves a far greater degree of activity than in the early days. Competition dancers, particularly in the Championship grades, use the floor to its best advantage, movement and projection being an integral part of their performance.

As with other forms of competitive dancing, the top class Champions have over the years become household names. Some have moved into other forms of dance, either competitively or on the stage. Others have gone into show business and many of the earlier Champions are now themselves successful teachers and choreographers.

It is interesting to note that the code of one-teacher-per-pupil remains and loyalty to each school is still strong. It is probably because of this that team events have remained very challenging and prestigious at the major festivals.

In 1991 saw Freestyle dance included in Le Classique de Danse Awards for the first time - the only time that recognition of this form of dance had been given. The Carl Alan Awards were reintroduced in 1993, with the inclusion of amateur and professional Freestyle categories.

We continue to see the constant improvement throughout all grades of competitive Freestyle dancers. This filters through to the medallist dancers, who continue to update on their work and extends upwards to the top Championship grade of dancer. The standard of our top competitors is now very high - excellent spins and splits, super high kicks, good choreography, superb presentation, projection and personality is now the norm.

There are a few events every year which attract the top class dancers where the standard, particularly at semi-final and final stage, is extremely strong and very hard fought in all age groups. The expertise of the younger dancer gets better all the time with some excellent Under 10 Years Championship Finals.

The United Kingdom Championships are organised by the ADFP and have in the past attracted dancers from Norway and South Africa as well as the best in the UK.

The British Freestyle Championships are held each year at the Wintergardens, Blackpool and are jointly organised by Leisure Parcs and D & A Jones. This is now a major event in the calendar and attracts a very good entry from across the country.

Each November sees a regular pilgrimage of the country's top dancers to the Midlands for the Dancer of the Year finals, organised by David and Anna Jones. The new outfits seem to surpass all previous costumes and the standard of dancing more than matches! 1993 saw the introduction of the first Slow Dance section at this event and qualifiers from each school were invited to take part. This was another dimension for these very talented young dancers and has since been introduced at many competitions throughout the year.

The Eurodance Championships are held at the Brean Sands festival every April. These are organised by Gary and Pat Waite and attract most of the top schools from England, Wales, Scotland and Ireland. This is normally a fun packed festival with top line demonstrations. Donnie Burns MBE, Gaynor Fairweather MBE and Marcus & Karen Hilton (both MBE) have topped the bill on at least two occasions and received a great reaction from this young and enthusiastic audience.

Nigel & Janice Horrocks also organize many successful competitions plus several large festivals which are regularly held at popular holiday camps in different parts of the country. They attract large entries of dancers in all sections, particularly in the team events.

The Universe Championships are held every summer in Birmingham and were organised by John Moase. (Since John's untimely death the championships have continued under the direction of Mrs June Moase.) This is a highly successful one day event attracting the country's top dancers and has often hosted very good competitors from abroad.

Barry Davids and Jeff Walker run very successful festivals each year whilst Bonnie Barr and David Johnson have been responsible for the running of many successful competitions and festivals in different parts of Scotland.

In 1994 "B & H Dance" organized a competition for adult dancers. Regional heats were held in night clubs across the UK. This was very well received, particularly as the winner's prize was an all expenses paid trip to America!

There are some excellent Sunday competitions held regularly throughout the country and most weekends have more than one event to choose from. Most promoters are now seasoned hands at organising a good day, and put as many as 50 events on the programme with non-returnable trophies going to all the finalists.

We have come a long way since *Night Fever* and continue to see an increase in the numbers of competitors and new professionals every year.

By continually working to improve the standard of teaching and performing with the use of good technique, as with any other form of dance its future will then be built on solid foundations.

SECTION 1 - DEMONSTRATION

It is important for any teacher of Freestyle dance to give some thought to the preparation of a well structured class.

The following is a brief plan starting with a limbering workout and moving onto various dance routines as suggested according to the grade of the pupils involved. Ideas for the exercises as well as the dances relevant to each level are included in this book.

The final routine should be followed by a "cool down" (See Exercise Section).

1)   A 32 bar exercise routine which is suitable for general limbering. (16 bars only for Students). As well as demonstrating this routine, the teacher should be able to step through each section and explain which muscles are being used and to what effect during its development.

2)   A medallist Freestyle routine (minimum 16 bars).
Student   =   Bronze/Beginner standard.
Associate   =   Silver/Intermediate standard.
Licentiate   =   Gold/Advanced standard.
Fellowship   =   Above Gold/Advanced standard

For Fellowship level the routine should be developed for a higher grade medal standard, e.g., "Bars and Stars" etc.. Keeping the original step pattern fairly constant but using changes of timing and/or different arm and hand movements etc.

3)   A Freestyle dance routine (minimum 16 bars) using the teachers own creative ability. Methods would be used in order to teach this routine that were not required when teaching the medal routine (e.g. body shaping, rhythmical interpretation etc.).

4)   For Fellowship only:- to teach and demonstrate for a minimum of $1\frac{1}{2}$ minutes a routine of varying rhythms. The teachers approach to this routine conveys their experience and understanding of the type of work they use. This routine may include dances with different time signature and tempos.

An example of Slow Dance must be included as one of the demonstration routines at Licentiate and Fellowship level (optional at Associate level).

SECTION 2 - DEFINITIONS

STUDENT
FREESTYLE DANCE
POSTURE
RHYTHM
TIME SIGNATURE
TEMPO
COUNTING IN BEATS & BARS
POISE
LOCOMOTIVE ACTION
NON-LOCOMOTIVE ACTION
PATTERN
ROUTINE
DIRECTIONAL CHART

ASSOCIATE
ACCENT
ACCENTED MOVEMENTS
PHRASE
RHYTHMICAL EXPRESSION
BALANCE

LICENTIATE
SYNCOPATION
POSITIONS OF FEET
AMOUNT OF TURN
FOOTWORK

FELLOWSHIP
BEAT
CHOREOGRAPHY
STACCATO
TIMING
DIRECTION
SPOTTING

FREESTYLE DANCE

Freestyle Dance is an artistic dance style that takes its roots from co-ordinating accentuated body movements together with a number of basic movements and steps incorporating arm, head and hand positions. This being controlled and developed by teachers taking into account modern trends and modern music, allowing the individual dancer freedom to express themselves from within these criteria to produce Freestyle dancing.

POSTURE

To stand with the feet slightly apart and naturally turned out. The weight will be equally distributed over the balls of the feet. The spine is stretched upward so that the breastbone tilts up slightly, carrying the whole chest to a slightly uplifted position. This stretch is continued through the neck to the head with the eyes facing forwards and the chin at a right angle to the neck.

RHYTHM

The regular occurrence or reoccurrence of an accented beat or beats in a bar of music.

TIME SIGNATURE

The number of beats in a bar of music and the value of each beat e.g.. 2/4 The digit above the line is the number of beats in the bar and the digit below the line is the value of each beat i.e.. crochet. The time signature of Freestyle is usually 2/4 or 4/4.

TEMPO

The speed of the music. This is measured as the number of beats or bars per minute.

COUNTING IN BEATS AND BARS

To count in beats and at the same time accumulate the numbers of bars e.g. 1234..2234..3234 etc.

POISE

Poise is the correct carriage of the body weight whether stationary, preparing to move or moving.

LOCOMOTIVE ACTION

Movements which involve travel e.g. Runs, Leaps, Progressive Spins.

NON-LOCOMOTIVE ACTION

Movements which are performed on the spot e.g.. Plié, Scuff, Twist turn.

PATTERN

A group of steps and movements which create various shapes either in the air and/or on the floor.

ROUTINE

A series of steps and movements.

DIRECTIONAL CHART

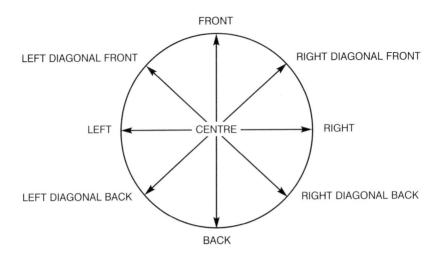

ASSOCIATE

ACCENT
The emphasis placed on a regular or irregular beat of music.

ACCENTED MOVEMENTS
Movements that are used to emphasise a particular piece of music, e.g., an 'explosion' or highlight could be used for a strong piece of music using, for example, a Leap or Box Splits Jump.

PHRASE
A distinct passage of music, e.g., a chorus.

RHYTHMICAL EXPRESSION
The way in which a dancer interprets the music by using their own methods of expressing their feelings through movement.

BALANCE
The correct distribution of the weight of the body over the feet.

LICENTIATE

SYNCOPATION
The irregular occurrence of an accented beat or beats in a bar of music. The accent is transferred to a part of the bar that has not been regularly accented. Because the basic rhythm has already been established, the variation produced does not cause rhythmical confusion.

THE NEXT 3 DEFINITIONS ARE IMPORTANT FOR THE INTERPRETATION OF SCRIPTS e.g. LECTURE NOTES.

POSITIONS OF FEET
The position of the moving foot in relation to the standing foot at the end of the step. e.g.. forwards, backwards, to side etc.

AMOUNT OF TURN
The amount of turn made by the body in relation to the room.

FOOTWORK
The part of the foot that is in contact with the floor during a particular step or movement.

FELLOWSHIP

BEAT
The basic rhythm of music i.e. The regular accented pulsation that makes the rhythm physically felt.

CHOREOGRAPHY
This is the art of arranging dance routines. Many different skills are required in Freestyle Dance to cater for Solo routines, Couples, Trios, Classwork, Teams, Slow and Street. Successful choreography is normally achieved by experience. The more work that a teacher can do over the years with the different forms of Freestyle will normally improve their ability to produce good routines that flow easily from one movement to the next and suit the individual dancer or dancers concerned. (See "Teaching Ability").

STACCATO
Music performed with the notes sharply separated. The dancer can then interpret this music with the use of acute steps and movements.

TIMING
This is the way in which we count the music. The normal way is 1234. We can slow down the movements by taking up 2 beats for each movement (or even slower if desired), i.e., 12=slow. Conversely, syncopate the timing by 'splitting' the beat and using the '&' count - 1&2. It is also possible to further split the beat - 1&a2. This is usually practicable in Slow Dance.
A combination of these different timings can also be used to create a more varied picture i.e. "light and shade". In 4/4 Time a step timed 'slow' occupies two beats of music. In 2/4 Time a 'slow' step occupies one beat, being equal to half a bar of music. (See also Teaching Ability).

DIRECTION

This refers to the movement of the dancer or dancers around the floor and is normally anti-clockwise.

SPOTTING

To focus the eyes on a fixed point in the room in order to spin in a straight line. The eyes will re-focus on this point upon each rotation. The head will ideally return to this position fractionally before the body on each turn. (See also "Spins"). It is also better to try and attain a horizontal position with the arms on the 'Spot' part of the turn.

SECTION 3 - SIMPLE ANATOMY
PHYSIOLOGY AND MECHANICS OF THE HUMAN BODY

ASSOCIATE

    ANATOMY

    PHYSIOLOGY

    THE SKELETAL SYSTEM

    THE MUSCULAR SYSTEM

    THE NERVOUS SYSTEM

    TENDONS

    CARTILAGE

    SYNOVIAL FLUID

    JOINTS & MOVEMENTS

    LIGAMENTS

LICENTIATE

    BONES

    MUSCLES

    THE RESPIRATORY SYSTEM (BREATHING)

FELLOWSHIP

    THE DIGESTIVE SYSTEM (FOOD & ENERGY)

    THE CARDIO-VASCULAR (CIRCULATORY) SYSTEM

All diagrams contained in this section have
been approved by a member of the medical profession.

SIMPLE ANATOMY
PHYSIOLOGY AND MECHANICS OF THE HUMAN BODY
ASSOCIATE

Anatomy and Physiology in dance are studied for three main reasons:-

1)   To enable us to achieve the best performance from a dancer.

2)   To know that we are not placing unreasonable demands upon the body of a dancer.

3)   To understand the precautions necessary to prevent physical injury either during preparation or performance.

ANATOMY

Anatomy is the detailed analysis of the structure of the body.

PHYSIOLOGY

Physiology is the study of the structure of body systems.

The systems of the body:- Skeletal, Digestive, Respiratory. Cardiovascular, Lymphatic, Urinary, Endocrine, Nervous, Reproductive plus the Muscular system. Only those directly affecting Dance and Exercise will be dealt with in this book.

THE SKELETAL SYSTEM

This consists of bones and cartilage. Its main function is support. It also protects the internal organs, provides muscle attachment by means of the tendons, acts as levers, produces red and white blood cells, stores calcium and phosphorus and gives characteristic shape to the body.

The Skeletal system along with the joints and muscles are known jointly as the Locomotor system.

THE MUSCULAR SYSTEM

This is comprised of Voluntary and Involuntary muscles. Its main functions are involved with stability and movement.

THE NERVOUS SYSTEM

This is comprised of the brain and nerves. It is the centre for sensation and intelligence and is responsible for the working of all the other body systems.

TENDONS

They are composed of tough bands of connective tissue. Tendons connect bone with muscle and by means of them, the pull of the muscle moves the bone. They are very strong and even when a bone is broken the tendon may remain undamaged.

CARTILAGE

A smooth polished covering found at the ends of each bone. It serves to break the force of concussion and enables the bones to glide smoothly against each other with the aid of synovial fluid.

Cartilage is found where rigidity and resilience are needed and at the joint surfaces, the front ends of the ribs and the supporting framework of trachea, bronchi, nose and ears.

The three main types of cartilage are:-

1)   Smooth hyaline.

2)   Tough-fibro.

3)   Elastic.

Cartilage cannot repair itself after injury and is replaced with fibrous scar tissue. Disuse leads towards the degeneration of cartilage, whereas activity aids the diffusion of nutrients.

SYNOVIAL FLUID

A yellowish viscid secretion of the synovial membrane which lubricates the joint thus allowing for free and easy movement.

JOINTS AND MOVEMENTS

Joints or articulations are formed when two bones or cartilages meet. They vary as regards mobility in different parts of the skeleton and some are quite immobile.

These are known as Synarthrodial joints, e.g. the bones of the skull.

In the movable joints known as Diarthrodial, the bones are covered with cartilage and held together by ligaments. They are lined throughout by the synovial membrane which secretes the synovial fluid thus providing lubrication for easy movement of the joint. The structures therefore that enter into the formation of a joint are bone, cartilage, fibro-cartilage, ligament and synovial membrane.

Fibro-cartilage consists of a mixture of white fibrous and cartilaginous tissues and is employed in the construction of joints by contributing to their strength and elasticity.

The main types of movable joint are:-

1)   Ball and Socket which is that form of joint which is capable of movement in all directions, i.e. round three axis, e.g. Shoulder and hip.

2)   Hinge joints which permit motion in one direction or plane only, i.e. forwards and backwards, e.g. Fingers, knees, toes, elbow and ankle.

3)   Pivot joints which are limited to a rotational mobility, e.g. Neck and elbow.

4)   Gliding joints which exhibit the simplest kind of motion and this is common to all movable joints, but in some cases is the only motion permitted, e.g. Shoulder blades, ankles and wrist.

5)   Condyloind joint, e.g. Wrist.   } Both are capable of
6)   Saddle joint, e.g. Thumb.   } movement round two axis.

N.B.   As can be seen, certain joints can fall into more than one category depending on the type of movement they exhibit.

LIGAMENTS

They are composed of bands of strong fibrous connective tissue and hold together the bones at a joint. Some ligaments are made of a white fibrous tissue which although not stretchable, are pliant enough to allow freedom of movement. Other ligaments are made of a yellow elastic tissue which are able to stretch. Ligaments can be over stretched due to undue force and/or misalignment rendering the joint more liable to dislocation.

LICENTIATE

BONES

Bones and Cartilage compose the Skeletal system. Bone is also a specialised tissue of mechanical function and is the hardest tissue in the body except for teeth. Its functions are listed under the heading "The Skeletal System".

There are four main types of bones:-

1)   Long bones e.g. Humerus (upper arm) and Femur (thigh).

2)   Short bones e.g. Carpals (wrist), Tapals (ankles) and the Vertebrae (spine).

3)   Flat bones e.g. Skull, ribs and scapula (shoulder blade).

4)   Sesamoid bones e.g.. Patella (knee-cap).

Bone is subject to compression, tension, twisting and bending strains and withstands these by its strength and elasticity. In old age and some diseases this strength is impaired and fractures can occur.

MUSCLES

Muscular tissue is composed of reddish muscle fibres arranged in bundles. Some muscles act as the result of conscious effort and others function unconsciously. Some only contract if stimulated by nerve impulses, some have an inherent pattern of contraction and others respond to circulating hormones.

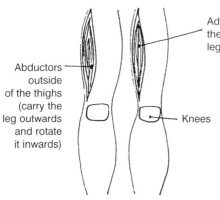

Adductors inside the tighs (pull the legs inwards)

Abductors outside of the thighs (carry the leg outwards and rotate it inwards)

Knees

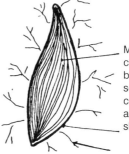

Muscles are composed of bundles of fibres seperated by connective tissue and wrapped in a sheath

There are three types of muscle:-

They depend on nerves which are attached to them. The nerves provide the stimulus which activates the muscle into action and causes it to change shape

1) Voluntry eg. Arm Muscle

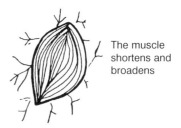

The muscle shortens and broadens

2) Involuntry eg. Abdomen

3) Cardiac ie. Heart

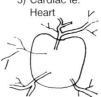

Copyright Anna Jones 1995

These varying functions are associated with different types of muscle structure:-

1)   Voluntary (striated, skeletal). These are found in the muscles attached to the skeleton and are under the conscious control of the central nervous system e.g. arm and leg muscles.

2)   Involuntary (unstriated, smooth). These form structures that must work automatically, beyond conscious control and regulated by the semi-independent autonomic nervous system e.g. abdomen and bladder.

3)   Cardiac i.e.. heart muscle. It occupies an intermediate situation as its fibres are striated but not under voluntary control.

The job of a muscle is to contract which causes it to shorten, harden and broaden thus drawing the moving bone to a fixed point.

Accurate balance and control of movement is achieved by the antagonistic action of the two opposing muscle groups - Flexors and Extensors.

Flexors bend or flex a limb by reducing the angle at a joint. Extensors straighten or extend a limb by increasing the angle at a joint.

Abductors are muscles that "take away" from the middle of the body i.e. those on the outside of the thighs which carry the leg outwards and rotate it inwards.

Adductors are muscles that draw towards the middle of the body i.e.. those on the inside of the thighs that pull the legs inwards.

Living muscle is never completely relaxed, except under deep anaesthesia, but is always in slight contraction which is called TONUS. This is essential to posture, particularly the erect posture, as it holds the body up against the strain of its own weight. In the feet and legs, the ligaments would be under enormous stresses but for the guarding of the surrounding muscles.

THE RESPIRATORY SYSTEM

This is commonly known as Breathing. It is the process by which oxygen enters the lungs, is transferred to the blood and circulated throughout the body and how carbon dioxide is carried in the blood to the lungs where it is then exhaled.

The lungs are the organ of respiration and are protected by the rib-cage. It is very important to breathe properly during dance and exercise as the need for oxygen uptake from respiration increases with the rate of exercise. During prolonged exercise the interchange of oxygen and CO_2 is so great that breathing through the mouth is also required but nasal breathing should be resumed as soon as possible as the nasal passages are properly equipped to warm, purify and dampen the air.

During a steady state of exercise the amount of oxygen taken up by the muscle is normally sufficient to meet the demand and this is the AEROBIC RESPIRATORY SYSTEM.

If there is insufficient oxygen to meet energy demand as at the start of intense exercise, substances in the muscle fibre break down to provide energy and this is the ANAEROBIC RESPIRATORY SYSTEM. The most important of these substances is glycogen, its waste product being lactic acid. If this accumulates in the muscle, as it may during static contraction, cramp and fatigue can develop.

It is important not to eat a large meal before dance or exercise because the increased activity results in more blood being required by the lungs. The digestive system would thus be deprived of enough blood to function properly and this can cause indigestion or abdominal pain known as stitch.

THE DIGESTIVE SYSTEM (FOOD AND ENERGY)

Protein, fat and carbohydrate are the fuels of the body. Any of these can be utilised for the production of energy, although proteins are not an economical way of obtaining energy.

Protein is an essential part of the diet because it provides the energy for growth and repair of tissue breakdown. It can be found in milk, cheese, eggs and fish etc. Any excess protein is not stored in the body but is broken down and excreted.

Carbohydrate is broken down into sugar and provides energy. Any excess is stored in the body as fat.

There are two types of carbohydrate:-

1) Refined carbohydrate e.g.. sugar and white flour. These are rapidly digested and absorbed producing great "peaks and troughs" in blood glucose levels.

2) Unrefined carbohydrate e.g. potatoes, wholemeal bread and brown rice. These are nutritionally more valuable than the refined carbohydrates and contain fibre and vitamin B. The latter helps convert starch into energy. Fibre helps to maintain a healthy digestive system and also creates a desirable balance of energy by assisting with the steady release of glucose into the bloodstream.

Fat provides energy and gives insulation to some of the organs. Like carbohydrate, excess fat is also stored in the body and is usually unwanted!

It can "fur up" the arteries causing heart disease, or much less dangerous but visibly unpleasant is cellulite where the fat collects under the skin giving a "dimpled" appearance. This often collects around the thighs and is more common in women than men. (The best way to reduce this is to eat less fat, drink more water and take more exercise). The average daily intake of fat is 30/35 grammes. Fat is found in butter, cream, cheese and meat.

There are two types of fat:-

1) Saturated i.e. animal fat which can increase a persons cholesterol level and ultimately make them more prone to heart disease.

2) Polyunsaturated i.e. vegetable fat which can actually reduce cholesterol.

A healthy diet is made up of the correct proportions of fat, protein and carbohydrate plus plenty of fresh food to ensure a good supply of vitamins and minerals. It is important to drink plenty of water, particularly when body fluids are being depleted faster than usual during and after dance or exercise. The average daily energy requirement is 3,000 calories for a man and 2,500 calories for a woman. (Sedentary workers require less).

THE CARDIOVASCULAR (CIRCULATORY) SYSTEM

This is a closed circle around which the blood is propelled by the contractions of the heart.

The main functions of the system are to transport:-

1) Oxygen from the lungs to all parts of the body.

2) Carbon dioxide from the body cells to the lungs for exhalation.

3) Nutrients to the body cells.

4) Waste from the body cells to the kidneys.

5) Excess heat through sweat glands to the skin surface where it evaporates, thus keeping the body temperature constant which is a very important function during dance and exercise.

There are two separate systems:-

1)` The systemic circulation which is driven by the left side of the heart and delivers blood to the body as a whole.

2)   The pulmonary circulation which is driven by the right side of the heart and is concerned with the passage of blood through the lungs.

The right and left side of the heart are separated from one another. Each has an upper chamber which receives blood from the veins and a lower chamber which pumps blood into arteries.

The arteries divide into smaller branches and finally break up into a meshwork of fine capillaries from where the blood discharges oxygen and food materials to the tissue cells. The network reforms to form small veins which become large venous trunks as they travel towards the heart. These are thin - walled, have no pulse and contain valves to prevent the backward flow of blood. Varicose veins are caused by the blood flowing slowly back up the legs against the force of gravity and causing strain on the valves. Foot and ankle movements are very useful to help combat varicose veins as they cause the muscles to pump the blood up the legs and back towards the heart.

SECTION 4 - EXERCISES

STUDENT
- INTRODUCTION
- IMPORTANT DO'S AND DON'TS
- WARM-UP
- COOLING DOWN
- BREATHING
- BREATHING EXERCISES
- ISOLATION EXERCISES:-
  - SHOULDERS AND ARMS
  - WRISTS
  - FINGERS
  - ELBOWS
  - NECK AND HEAD
  - HIPS
  - KNEES
  - ANKLES AND FEET
- SIMPLE COMBINATION EXERCISE

ASSOCIATE
- ISOLATION EXERCISES:-
  - PELVIS/LOWER BACK
  - SIDES/WAIST
  - CHEST
  - SPINE
- ADVANCED COMBINATION EXERCISE

LICENTIATE
- ISOLATION EXERCISES:-
  - THIGHS
  - QUADS
  - CALF
  - HAMSTRINGS
- FLOORWORK EXERCISES

FELLOWSHIP
- GENERAL EXERCISES:-
  - UPPER BODY x 2
  - LOWER BODY x 2
  - BACK BENDS
  - ABDOMINALS
- CARDIO EXERCISE
- FLOOR EXERCISE FOR TRICEPS, POSTERIOR AND THIGHS
- FURTHER ADVANCED COMBINATION EXERCISE

EXERCISES

STUDENT

INTRODUCTION
It is important that appropriate clothing and footwear be worn for exercising. 100% cotton clothing allows the skin to "breathe", Lycra^S or cotton allows freedom of movement. Shoes should be flexible but also provide support and protection.

IMPORTANT DO'S AND DON'TS
1) Do not eat less than 3 hours prior to abdominal exercise. (If this is not possible, keep to very light foods such as fresh fruit).
2) Never throw leg or arm movements against the joint as this could result in tissue injury.
3) With exercise that involves kicks, ensure that the muscles around the joint are relaxed.
4) Avoid the danger of rupture (hernia) which can be caused if strong abdominal contractions are encouraged without due care in training.
5) Be very careful of spinal damage. This can be caused in several ways, some of the most common mistakes are:-
   a) Sudden forward bending movements of the trunk, especially with the breath held.
   b) Double leg raising - this used to be advocated for strengthening stomach muscles but is now known to be very dangerous.
   c) Sit-ups with a straight back - causes similar effects as the double leg raising and should always be avoided.

WARM UP
The human body cannot be expected to jump directly into top gear from a resting position. It is essential that the work to be done by the heart and lungs is gradually increased and that the body becomes more flexible so as to reduce the risk of injury to the muscles, joints, ligaments and tendons.

Movements should be used that promote the flow of blood to the working muscles e.g. Swinging, swaying, shaking and rhythmical exercises. The movements involved should naturally flow from one to another and gradually increase in intensity.

Jogging on the spot or around the room is a good way to start. This can then be followed by a variety of exercises that will satisfy the requirements of a good "warming up" session e.g. "jumping - jacks", "grapevine", arm swings, shoulder movement, plies, hip circles etc..

Remember that all stretches should be counteracted with relaxation to ensure the release of tension.

COOLING DOWN
A "cool down" aims to gradually return the body physically and mentally from a state of high activity to a non-exercising condition.

Movements should endeavour to relax the body and release muscle tension. Gentle swaying and shaking should be included in order to help the return of blood from the extremities back to the heart.

Movements need to be easy, rhythmical and flowing and gradually "wind down" to a slower degree until almost at a standstill.

A good "cool down" will also help to relieve muscle stiffness and to aid the diffusion of lactic acid. See also "The Respiratory System".

Suggested Breathing Exercise as an aid for Cooling Down:-

Starting with hands down at sides, breathe in slowly whilst lifting arms high above head to the count of 1234. Hold this position for 4 more beats with the breath held in, then slowly exhale and lower arms back down to the sides to the count of 1234. Hold this position for 4 more beats with the breath out and then repeat. The tempo of the music can be gradually lowered as the breathing returns to normal.

BREATHING

It is very important to breathe correctly at all times and particularly during dance and exercise as the body then requires a greater amount of oxygen. This subsequently means a faster expulsion of Carbon Dioxide (CO_2) so that the interchange is very great as more exercise or dance is performed and therefore our mode of breathing alters. (See also "The Respiratory System")

During Freestyle dance at medium to fast tempos it is necessary to maintain regular breathing and not to hold ones breath at all during a performance as this will not allow the dancer to achieve the best results. It can make the dancer look as if they are not finishing-off their movements correctly because they are always striving to get to the end of the performance in order to breathe again. It is usually necessary to breathe through the mouth as well as the nose to maintain the level of oxygen required. Nasal breathing should then be resumed as soon as possible.

During "Slow Freestyle Dance" a different method can be adopted whereby the breathing can be used to specifically aid the production of a particular movement by drawing the breath in slowly in order to achieve expansion and extension. Conversely a gradual exhalation can assist the relaxation of muscles which is required to achieve other types of movements.

In contrast to this, when performing certain exercises of a repetitive nature e.g. many of those used during circuit training in a gymnasium, it is correct to exhale on the effort and inhale on the relaxation. This method can be used on some of the more strenuous exercises that follow in particular those involving the floorwork.

BREATHING EXERCISES

1) With hands on abdomen and fingers touching, breath in so that the stomach expands and the finger tips slightly come apart. Continue to breathe in filling the lungs further, and expanding the lower part of the chest. Raising the middle part of the chest, slightly contract the stomach and continue to breathe in. Finally lift and expand the lower ribs to fill the top part of the lungs before slowly releasing the breath.

2) Extend arms forward at chest level. Breathe in whilst drawing the hands inwards towards the chest with the fists clenched at the same time expanding the chest. Hold the breath for a few seconds then breathe out, relaxing the hands and arms back down to the sides.

3) Breathe in whilst rising onto toes, pushing the shoulders backwards and downwards. Hold the position for a few seconds then relax and breathe out whilst lowering the heels to the floor and allowing the shoulders to droop.

4) Breathing whilst relaxed or reclined.

ISOLATION EXERCISES

These are movements which single out or separate individual parts of the body independently of
the others. The following are suggested isolation exercises for different parts of the
body. Other suitable alternatives are also acceptable for examination purposes.

SHOULDERS AND ARMS

1) Clapping hands in front and behind body.
2) Pull elbows back with arms flexed or straight or a combination of the two.
3) Lifting, dropping and circling of the shoulders, forwards or backwards either one at a
   time or both together.
4) Moving shoulders forwards and backwards.
5) Arm circles with the arms straight, forwards or backwards, either one at a time or both
   together.
6) Arm circles in a clockwise or anti-clockwise direction with arms straight and parallel.
7) Circling of the lower arms from the elbows in a clockwise and anticlockwise direction.

WRISTS

Lifting, dropping, circling and shaking of the hands.

FINGERS

Clenching and stretching of the fingers and the "piano exercise".

ELBOWS

1) Swing forearms from side to side
2) Circle the forearms.   } Keeping the upper
3) Curl the forearms upwards   arm extended and still.
   and then extend them downwards.

NECK AND HEAD

Nodding head forwards and upwards (but not backwards), turning from side to side and half
circling. Head should never be rotated behind the facial line.

HIPS

1) Swing the whole leg forwards and backwards from the hip.
2) Sit on floor with the soles of feet together and gently press the knees downwards
   towards the floor. (Do not over exert as this can cause groin strain).
3) Hip swings/rocks, bumps, circles, lifts and figures of eight.

KNEES

1) Move the lower leg forwards and backwards keeping the thigh still.
2) Flex and straighten the knees. (Pliés). } Both also useful for exercising
3) Lunge lines into each leg.   } the groin and the Quads.
4) Lift right knee at the same time taking right elbow down to the outside of the knee,
   repeat taking elbow down to the inside of the knee and then repeat with left knee and
   elbow.

ANKLES AND FEET

1) Lifting, dropping and circling of the feet. This is particularly beneficial to help against varicose veins.
2) Rise onto the ball and then onto the toes of one foot.
3) Rise slowly onto the balls of both feet then slowly lower and rock back onto the heels. (Also useful to exercise calf muscles).
4) 'Pony Trots' through the feet.
5) Clenching and stretching of the toes.

SIMPLE COMBINATION EXERCISE (8 Bars)

MOVEMENTS   *COUNT*

Commencing feet apart with weight on both feet, swing hips from side to side
moving to the right or left first.   1-8
Continue to swing the hips from side to side and starting with the right or left
arm turn the wrist and elbow at shoulder level. Repeat with the other arm
and continue to alternate.   1-8
Continue to swing the hips and alternate the turning of the arms whilst also turning
the head from left-to-right or right-to-left alternately.   1-8
Keeping the head still, continue to swing the hips and also sweep the arms down
to cross in front of body then up into High V and continue to alternate.   1-8

ASSOCIATE

ISOLATION EXERCISES
PELVIS/LOWER BACK
With the knees flexed tilt the pelvis forwards and backwards.

SIDES/WAIST

1) Stretch the arm and side upwards, right and left alternately then lean sideways with right arm leaning to the left and left arm leaning to the right.
2) Turn the body from the waist to right and left alternately to look behind.

CHEST

1) Move the ribcage from side to side.
2) Move the ribcage forwards and backwards.
3) Circling of the ribcage.
4) With the hands joined behind the back lift the arms to a comfortable position with the palms facing inwards.

SPINE

1) Arms stretching above head with one hand high then the other, as if climbing a ladder.
2) Sit on the floor with legs apart, spine stretched upwards and arms in high parallel position. Stretch forwards over the right leg and return into an upward stretch then stretch forwards over the left leg and return into an upward stretch. Finally, stretch forwards between both legs and return to the upward stretch. Keep the spine straight throughout the exercise and only perform these movements when fully warmed-up.

ADVANCED COMBINATION EXERCISE (18 Bars)

MOVEMENTS

COUNT

Start with feet apart, weight on both feet.	
Rise onto ball of right foot, then up onto the toe.	12
Lower to ball and flat.	34
Repeat first bar on left foot.	1-4
Flick, ball, tap on right foot.	1&2
Flick and change on left foot.	34
Repeat previous bar.	1-4
Four bounces with feet apart, tilt the pelvis slightly backwards and forwards.	1-4
Repeat previous bar.	1-4
Swing hips from side to side, starting to the right.	1-4
Repeat previous bar.	1-4
Touch floor with both hands. (knees slightly flexed).	1
Touch shoulders with both hands.	2
Stretch both arms straight upwards.	3
Touch shoulders with both hands.	4
Repeat previous bar.	1-4
Move shoulders backwards and forwards twice.	1-4
Repeat previous bar.	1-4
Circle right arm backwards twice.	1-4
Repeat previous bar.	1-4
Circle left arm backwards twice.	1-4
Repeat previous bar.	1-4
Lower head.	12
Raise head.	34
Turn head to the left.	12
Turn head to the right.	34

ISOLATION EXERCISES
THIGHS
Kneel upright with hands on sides of head, incline body slowly backwards in one movement and return to the upright position keeping the spine straight throughout.

QUADS (Front of upper leg)
Bend right leg upwards behind body by lifting from the ankle with the right hand. Extend leg slightly back from the body for further stretch. Repeat with the left leg.

CALF
Extend the right leg backwards keeping it straight with both feet parallel and heels on the floor, left knee flexed. Repeat on the left leg.

HAMSTRINGS
Lying down with back flat on the floor, raise right leg with knee flexed. Keeping the foot flat and parallel to the ceiling, grip the calf with the right hand and support back of thigh with the left hand, gently straighten knee. Hold for 10 seconds. Repeat on the left leg.

FLOORWORK EXERCISES
1) Lying down with back flat on floor and hands on sides of head (not behind head), bend and lift both knees towards head at the same time lifting head and shoulders towards the knees. Then lower and repeat. For effective "sit-ups" it is only necessary for the head and shoulders to raise slightly off the floor so that the stretch is felt in the abdominal muscles but no strain is put on the spine i.e., Crunch.
2) Kneeling with legs parallel and close together and hands on floor at shoulder width, hump and hollow the back in order to expand and contract the abdominal muscles. This also exercises the middle spine region.
3) The "cat stretch":-
(a) lie on stomach with hands facing downwards under the shoulders and push the body gently upwards and backwards raising the bottom up first to finish sitting on ankles. Return to the starting position by lowering the chest first and the bottom down last, or
(b) commence on both knees, sitting back on heels, arms fully extended forward with the palms of the hands resting on the floor, feeling the stretch from the base of the spine to the finger tips. Lower the face towards the floor by bending arms and transferring the weight forwards until lying face down, both legs now fully stretched, hands under shoulders with the elbows tucked in. Raise the head and with pressure straighten the arms until the back is arched (a catlike shape) hips remain in contact with the floor. Return to kneeling position, hands stay in place - press middle of the back up to concave shape. Sit back to commencing position.
4) To improve kicks:- lie on side and kick leg up with turnout and/or hold the ankle and gently extend the leg. Repeat on the other side.
5) To improve front splits:- Extend slowly into deep lunge with front heel on the floor, then lower into full splits or half splits with turnout of the back foot. (With one hand either side of front leg, palms on the floor.)
6) To improve box splits:- Squat on the floor with feet together and body weight slightly forwards then extend legs fully out to either side of body. (With both hands in front of body, palms on the floor.)

FELLOWSHIP

GENERAL EXERCISES:
UPPER BODY
1) Stand with legs apart and knees slightly flexed. Stretch arms forward in parallel position with palms facing each other. Swing both arms out wide to horizontal position at shoulder height and then return to starting position. Build up to 20 repetitions.

2) Stand with legs apart and knees slightly flexed. Flex elbows and bring hands up to shoulders, palms facing inwards. Punch upwards with one fist and bring it back down to shoulder level as the other fist is punched upwards. Build up to 20 repetitions with each arm. Then punch upwards with both fists together, 20 times.

LOWER BODY
1) Stand with feet apart and legs straight. Keep arms straight by sides with palms facing inwards. Lift both arms high above head at the same time flexing knees. Keeping the back straight, move into a squat position. Return arms to starting position, at the same time straightening legs. Build up to 20 repetitions.

2) Stand with feet apart and legs straight. Hold both arms down in front of body with palms facing the body. Flex knees into squat position and lift arms above head. Then straighten the legs and bring arms back down to starting position. Build up to 20 repetitions.

BACK BENDS
With feet apart, bend body forwards from the waist whilst making the 'breast-stroke' movement with both arms. Then place hands on lower back and bend slightly backwards from the waist with head raised. Repeat four times.

ABDOMINALS
Lie flat on back, feet flat on the floor and knees flexed. Press lower back into the floor and place hands behind head. Exhale and slowly raise shoulders off the floor by contracting the abdominal muscles. Inhale and lower the body back down to the floor. Keep the head relaxed and chin off the chest. Gradually build up the number of repetitions.

CARDIO EXERCISE
Kneel down with hands, knees and feet in contact with the floor. Keep the arms shoulder-width apart with hands flat on the floor pointing forwards. Lift knees off the floor, one at a time straightening legs, keeping the back and shoulders level with posterior. Release the right foot from the floor and bring the right knee up toward the chest. Then straighten right leg and return to starting position. Repeat three times. Repeat exercise with left leg.

FLOOR EXERCISES FOR TRICEPS, POSTERIOR AND THIGHS
Sit on the floor with knees flexed and feet flat, palms down with fingers pointing forwards. Keeping the back straight, lift the posterior off the floor whilst straightening right leg out in front parallel to the floor with toes pointing forward. Keeping the leg straight, lift foot upwards as if performing a high kick. Return to starting position. Repeat three times. Repeat exercise with left leg.

FURTHER ADVANCED COMBINATION EXERCISE (20 Bars)

MOVEMENTS	COUNT
Standing with feet apart, weight on both feet, rotate arms outwards from the elbows three times.	1-3
Stretch both arms outwards into a horizontal position.	4
Repeat previous bar.	1-4
Lean leftwards from the waist with both arms parallel above head.	12
Return to upright position with arms at sides, elbows flexed and hands upwards fists clenched.	34
Repeat previous bar.	1-4
Repeat previous 2 bars, leaning to the right and returning to upright position.	1-4, 1-4
Extend right leg backwards, press lightly down onto ball of foot with arms stretched forwards, hands clasped.	1-4
Repeat previous bar.	1-4
Return right foot to side of left foot and walk on the spot.	1-4
Extend left leg backwards, press lightly down onto ball of foot with arms stretched forwards, hands clasped.	1-4
Repeat previous bar.	1-4
Return left foot to side of right foot and walk on the spot.	1-4
Lower into right knee with left leg extended to side and both hands on the floor.	12
Turn body ? to right and move hands in front of body, both still touching the floor	34
Straighten both knees.	12
Stand up straight with feet slightly apart	34
Repeat previous 2 bars, lowering into left knee, turning and straightening up.	1-4, 1-4
Circle both arms outwards twice.	1-4
Lunge slightly into right knee and lift right shoulder.	1
Lunge slightly into left knee and lift left shoulder	2
Repeat previous 12.	34
Extend both arms upwards with hands clasped.	1
Bring hands down to waist.	2
Touch floor with both hands. (Knees slightly flexed).	3
Stand up straight.	4
Repeat previous bar.	1-4

N.B.   All 3 combination exercises should be performed at a steady tempo so that the movements can be fully completed.

SECTION 5 - STEPS AND MOVEMENTS

Note: An amalgamation of three steps/movements from the Associate syllabus
will be required in all grades for examination purposes.

STUDENT
STEP
PRESSURE STEP
WALK
SHOULDER WALKS
RUN
STRIDE
JUMP
HOP
SPIN
TURN
OPEN TURN
CHASSÉ

ASSOCIATE
PLIÉ
DEMI PLIÉ
SWITCH TURN
WHISK TURN
CROSS TURN
TWIST TURN
FLICK
KICK
BALL CHANGE
KICK/FLICK BALL CHANGE
STAMP
SCUFF
STOMP
BRUSH
LUNGE
DEVELOPPÉ
SPIRAL
TAP
SPRING
CROSS -TAP KICK

LICENTIATE
* FULL SPLITS
* HALF SPLITS
* BOX SPLITS
* BOX SPLITS JUMP
* STAR JUMP
* ATTITUDE JUMP
* LEAP
* STAG LEAP
* SCISSORS LEAP
* SCISSORS KICK
* SPRING KICK
* DROP OR HITCH KICK
PIROUETTE
ARABESQUE
ATTITUDE
SLIDE

FELLOWSHIP
PIVOT
RONDÉ
BOTAFOGO
LAZY BOTAFOGO
PROGRESSIVE SPINS
ACCELERATED SPINS
RELEVÉ
JETÉ
* SPLITS LEAP
* FORWARD KICK LEAP
*SIDE KICK LEAP
* SCISSORS OR CRISS CROSS JUMP
ROTATIONAL HOP
TOUR
PIVOT KICK
CHECK
PLAIT ACTION
* ROTATIONAL PIVOT

* These steps and movements will not be required to be
demonstrated but they must be clearly described and understood.

STEPS AND MOVEMENTS

STUDENT

STEP
A movement of one foot taken in any direction with weight transference.

PRESSURE STEP
A movement of one foot taken in any direction without weight transference. The step is taken with pressure into the floor, partial weight being retained on the supporting foot.

WALK
A weight transference from one foot to the other whilst moving in any direction. Both feet are close to the floor and one foot is always in contact with the floor. It is important to continue the development of a good walk action. The weight of the body should be held over the balls of the feet, with the chest and head uplifted. Forward walks are normally performed with the balls of the feet in contact with the floor first. However, heel leads can be used to achieve a different effect although the body weight should not be allowed to drop back. Backward walks are normally achieved by rolling through the feet from the ball to the heel with the release of the front heel as the back heel lowers. However, the toe of the front foot can be released first as the back heel lowers in order to achieve a different effect. Foot pressure into the floor is most important to produce strength through the ankles and legs. Walks can also be performed sideways or diagonally. Many varied arm movements can be used for walks in each direction.

SHOULDER WALKS
A rolling movement of each shoulder, usually commenced in a backward direction, corresponding simultaneously with the forward or backward walk on each foot, i.e., same side shoulder as foot on each walk.

RUN
A weight transference from one foot to the other whilst moving in any direction, the legs travelling faster than when walking.

STRIDE
A 'stretched' run whereby each leg is, in turn, extended further than on a normal run.

JUMP
Elevation of the body upwards with both feet leaving the floor, landing on one or both feet simultaneously with flexing of the knees and ankles. (Quote from Wayne Sleep - "Anybody can jump, only the best can land.")

HOP
Elevation of the body upwards from one foot landing on the same foot with flexing of the knees and ankles. This can be performed on the spot or with progression in any direction.

SPIN
A rotation to left or right on the spot or travelling. It is normally performed on the ball of the foot. (See also, Pirouette, Pivot, Progressive Spins and Accelerated Spin).

TURN

A revolving movement normally incorporating a series of steps with or without progression. (See also Open Turn, Switch Turn, Whisk Turn, Cross Turn, Twist Turn and Spiral).

OPEN TURN

A three step movement turning continuously to right or left.

CHASSÉ

A three step movement in any direction, closing or almost closing the feet on the second step.

ASSOCIATE

PLIÉ

A flexing and straightening of the knees. The knees aligned with feet.

DEMI PLIÉ

A plié taken with only slight flexing and straightening of the knees.

SWITCH TURN

A step forward onto the right foot followed by half a turn to the left with weight transference onto the left foot. Can be commenced on left foot turning to right. Amount of turn may vary slightly.

WHISK TURN

A step to side on the right foot normally taken with a slight spring action followed by left foot crossed behind right foot with part weight, knees slightly flexed. A turn to the left is then made on the balls of both feet. When half a turn is made the feet finish apart and the weight is usually equal between both feet. When a full turn is made the feet re-cross and the weight is usually transferred to the left foot. Can be commenced on left foot. Can also be used as a travelling movement.

CROSS TURN

A step to the side on the right foot normally taken with a slight spring action followed by left foot crossed in front of right foot with part weight, knees slightly flexed. A turn to the right is then made on the balls of both feet. When half a turn is made the feet finish apart and the weight is usually equal between both feet. When a full turn is made the feet re-cross and the weight is usually transferred to the left foot. Can be commenced on left foot. Amount of turn can be varied.

TWIST TURN

Commenced with left foot in front of right foot, a rise onto the toes is followed by half a turn to the right when the feet then lower and recross. A further rise onto the toes is then followed by half a turn to the left when the feet then lower and recross. Can be commenced with right foot in front of left foot. Amount of turn can be varied. Can also be danced without 'rise'.

FLICK

A brisk movement of the lower leg from the knee in any direction.

KICK
A movement of the whole leg from the hip in any direction.

BALL CHANGE
A change of weight from the ball of one foot onto the ball or flat of the other foot.

KICK/FLICK BALL CHANGE
A kick or flick of the right foot followed by a small step back onto the ball of the right foot with part weight and then a small step forward or on the spot onto the left foot. Can be commenced on left foot. May also be danced in reverse i.e. Ball Change Kick/Flick.

STAMP
The placing of either foot with firm pressure onto the floor producing a heavy sound with the foot flat. Can be performed with or without weight.

SCUFF
A "moving stamp" that normally ends with a stretched foot.

STOMP
A short sharp forward push or shunt into the floor on one or both feet with slight flexing of the knees.

BRUSH
A swing of the leg using the hip and knee joint, either forwards or backwards, the ball of the moving foot in contact with the floor as it passes the supporting foot.

LUNGE
A step taken in any direction on either foot with the weight held over the flexed supporting leg, leaving the other leg extended.

DEVELOPPÉ
To unfold either leg in any direction whilst standing on the other foot.

SPIRAL
A turn on the ball of one foot with the other foot held loosely in front without weight.

TAP
A light contact with the floor on either foot using the toe or ball of foot without weight transference.

SPRING
A light elevation of the body from one foot landing on the opposite foot with flexing of the knees and ankles.

CROSS-TAP KICK
Step right foot forward and across left foot (count 1). Extend left foot to side without weight (count 2). Step left foot forward and across right foot (count 3). Raise right leg into kick (count 4). Can be commenced on left foot and finished with a left leg kick.

LICENTIATE

FULL SPLITS*
One leg extended fully forwards and the other extended fully backwards with both legs parallel to the floor and the body facing direction of front leg.

HALF SPLITS*
One leg extended forwards and the other leg extended backwards with the knee slightly flexed and the body facing direction of front leg. (Sometimes referred to as 'American Splits'.)

BOX SPLITS*
Both legs fully extended to either side of body with both legs parallel to the floor. Body facing forwards.

BOX SPLITS JUMP* ("FAME" JUMP)
A spring into the air from both feet into box splits position with arms parallel to legs. commencing and landing with flexing of the knees and ankles.

STAR JUMP*
A spring into the air from both feet with arms and legs extending to form the shape of an "X". Commencing and landing with flexing of the knees and ankles.

ATTITUDE JUMP*
A high jump with the flexing of both knees, one leg in front and one leg behind the body. Commencing and landing with flexing of the knees and ankles.

LEAP*
An elevation of the whole body forwards or sideways which is usually taken from a travelling movement with progression. A leap is normally taken from a run to gain height and extension. All leaps should land with flexing of the knees and ankles. (Can also be danced from a stationary position.)

STAG LEAP*
A leap into the air flexing the front leg under the body whilst extending the other leg backwards with the knee straight.

SCISSORS LEAP*
A difficult figure which requires a leap forward in splits position and then reversing the splits position whilst still in the air.

SCISSORS KICK*
A step forward on the right foot followed by a swing into a front high kick with the left leg and then a kick into a front high kick with the right leg so that the legs pass each other in the air. Landing on the left leg with slight flexing of the knee. Can be commenced on the left foot.

SPRING KICK*
A spring onto the balls of both feet followed by a spring onto the ball of one foot throwing the other leg upwards into a front kick.

DROP OR HITCH KICK*

With weight on right foot, a drop into the left leg with flexing of the knee and simultaneously kicking of the right leg into a front high kick. Can be commenced on left foot.

PIROUETTE

A step into a spin either to right or left on one foot with the other foot released from the floor. (Stepping right foot forward and spinning to the right will be an outward pirouette whilst stepping right foot forward and spinning to left will be an inward pirouette and vice versa).

ARABESQUE

To stand on one leg with the other leg extended backwards, (derrière) the rear foot either raised or in contact with the floor and the body erect. The leg without weight can also be extended forwards with the front foot either raised or in contact with the floor (devant).

ATTITUDE

To stand on one leg with the other leg held forwards, sideways or backwards with the knee flexed at approximately right angles to the thigh.

SLIDE

A slipping movement taken on one or both feet which is brought about by the projection of the body forwards and ending with the body poised backwards. Also used to describe the closing of the moving foot towards the standing foot whilst keeping the moving foot in contact with the floor.

FELLOWSHIP

PIVOT

To rotate on one foot whilst the other foot is held in a set position.

RONDÉ

An upward and outward rotation of the leg from the knee and hip.

BOTAFOGO

A step taken across the body on the right foot followed by a "ball change" movement onto the left foot using a side step with part weight and then a replacement of weight onto the right foot in place. Can be commenced on left foot. (Usually timed 1&2.)

LAZY BOTAFOGO

A step taken across the body on the right foot followed by an extension of the left foot to the side without weight transference. Can be commenced on the left foot. (Usually timed 1,2.) Can be danced with different effects, e.g., (a) at normal height, (b) low into flexed knees with finger clicks, (c) with syncopated shoulder movements (shoulders timed 1&2).

PROGRESSIVE SPINS

A series of spins using alternative feet travelling in a straight line across or around the floor. The technique of "spotting" should be used to achieve top quality spins.

ACCELERATED SPINS
Progressive spins that gradually increase in speed (usually timed 1234&5&6&7&8), i.e., to syncopate the timing of steps 4 to 8 by splitting the beat and doubling the number of steps.

RELEVÉ
A rise through the feet brought about by lifting the heels from the floor and transferring the weight onto the balls or toes of the feet. Can be performed on one or both feet.

JETÉ
Propulsion of the body weight from one foot to the other in any direction. (Direction is more laterally than upwards.)

SPLITS LEAP*
A leap into the air extending front leg forwards with rear leg extended backwards or flexed in attitude. (The latter is opposite to the Stag Leap).

FORWARD KICK LEAP*
A spring into the air extending front leg forwards with launching leg flexed back. Both arms maybe extended forwards in parallel position which is different to the Splits Leap, Stag Leap and Scissors Leap in which the arms are normally either in a high 'V' or in opposition. The launching leg can alternatively be raised towards the extended leg. This can also be danced sideways (SIDE KICK LEAP*) in which case the arms are normally extended into horizontal position.

SCISSORS OR CRISS-CROSS JUMP*
A spring into the air passing both feet forwards and backwards past each other (RLR) or (LRL) before landing with flexing of the knees and ankles.

ROTATIONAL HOP
A series of hops onto the same foot turning continuously with the free leg extended or flexed.

TOUR
A jump involving turn. A full Tour involves one complete turn having been made on landing. More or less turn can be made. Landing with flexing of knees and ankles.

PIVOT KICK
A pivot turn followed by a flick or kick using the free leg. Can also be danced as a flick or kick then pivot turn.

CHECK
A step taken on the right foot in any direction with only part weight transfer. Weight is then transferred back onto the ball of the left foot and the right foot is then returned to its original position This is normally danced as a fast movement timed 1 and 2. Can be commenced on left foot.

PLAIT ACTION
A swivelling movement of the feet whereby the moving foot sweeps towards and then away from the standing foot. A series of swivels are normally performed using alternate feet. This action can be danced as a locomotive or non-locomotive action.

ROTATIONAL PIVOT*

A continual hop on the left leg making several turns on the spot in a clockwise direction whilst flicking the right leg outwards and inwards with a slight rondé action. Can be performed on the opposite leg whilst turning in an anti-clockwise direction.

—-ooo000ooo—-

SAMPLE QUESTIONS FOR ALL GRADES

A few examples of the type of questions that one should be prepared for are as follows:-

1) Demonstrate the WALK action in 3 different ways to include varying arm and shoulder movements.

2) Display at least 2 types of RUN using different directions and use of arms.

3) Describe and/or demonstrate at least 3 different types of JUMP/LEAP and explain how they can be developed.

4) Having taught or performed the SPLITS describe and/or demonstrate at least 3 different ways of returning to an upright position, e.g. to bring both legs in front of the body with the feet about "shoulder width" apart. Push the body upwards with the knees flexed, abdomen in advance and head up last.

5) Explain how you would develop a SPIN to travel down the floor i.e. progressive spins (to incorporate teaching methods).

6) Explain at least 3 different timings and/or interpretations of the OPEN TURN.

7) Can you suggest a way in which the TWIST TURN could be developed for more advanced dancers?

8) Demonstrate at least 3 different types of CHASSÉ using varying timings and/or arm movements.

9) Demonstrate at least 3 different ways of incorporating the BALL CHANGE into routines of varying grades.

10) Give 2 precedes and follows to the BOTAFOGO.

11) Perform a short amalgamation of at least 3 of the steps and/or movements in the syllabus.

SECTION 6 - HEAD, ARM,
HAND AND BODY MOVEMENTS

STUDENT

HEAD POSITIONS
    ERECT
    TURNED
    INCLINED
    TURNED & INCLINED
    RAISED
    LOWERED
    HEAD ROLL/HALF CIRCULAR MOVEMENTS

ARM POSITIONS & MOVEMENTS
    HORIZONTAL
    PARALLEL
    DIAGONAL
    OPPOSITION
    HIGH V
    LOW V
    ARM CIRCLES
    WRIST CIRCLES
    PUSHING
    PULLING
    ARM SWINGS

HAND POSITIONS & MOVEMENTS (1-9)

ASSOCIATE

BODY MOVEMENTS:
    CONTRACTION
    RELAXATION
    MIDDLE BODY MOVEMENT
    RIB CAGE MOVEMENT
    SHOULDER MOVEMENT
    BODY BENDING
    SWAY
    BOUNCE
    SHAKE
    BODY STRETCHING
    RHYTHMICAL BODY ACTION
    EXPANSION

LICENTIATE

BODY MOVEMENTS:
- CIRCULAR ACTION
- PELVIC ACTION
- HIP ACTION
- MERENGUE ACTION
- FOOT AND LEG ACTION
- RIPPLE
- UPWARD BODY RIPPLE
- DOWNWARD BODY RIPPLE
- * FORWARD ROLL

* This movement will not be required to be demonstrated
        but must be clearly described and understood.

HAND HOLDS USED IN COUPLES WORK

CONTEMPORARY ARM & HAND MOVEMENTS

FELLOWSHIP

- JAZZ-LINE
- CONTRA BODY MOVEMENT (CBM)
- CONTRA BODY MOVEMENT POSITION (CBMP)
- HUG HOLD
- FLOOR WORK
- FOOT POSITIONS

HEAD, ARM , HAND AND BODY MOVEMENTS

STUDENT

HEAD POSITIONS
There are six standard positions of the head:-

1)   ERECT i.e. facing forwards with the chin at a right angle to the neck.

2)   TURNED i.e. facing either to right or left.

3)   INCLINED i.e. tilted from the vertical position.

4)   TURNED & INCLINED

5)   RAISED i.e. lifted upwards.

6)   LOWERED i.e. facing downwards.

7)   HEAD ROLL/HALF CIRCULAR MOVEMENT
      This is commenced by turning the head to either side then lowering the chin and allowing the head to circle in a downward direction to complete a half circle.
      It is dangerous to rotate the head in an upward direction as this can cause damage to the spine. Movements of this type should therefore be discouraged.

ARM POSITIONS & MOVEMENTS
1)   HORIZONTAL - both arms stretched outwards at shoulder height parallel to the floor.

2)   PARALLEL - Both arms carried in the same direction as each other and being equidistant.

3)   DIAGONAL - One arm stretched high and the other low in opposite directions to each other at any level.

4)   OPPOSITION - Arms carried in opposite directions to each other i.e. one arm forwards and the other backwards at any level.

5)   HIGH V - Both arms stretched upwards and outwards.

6)   LOW V - Both arms stretched downwards and outwards.

7)   ARM CIRCLES - The circling of one or both arms in any direction from either the shoulders or the elbows.

8)   WRIST CIRCLES - The continuous circling of either one or both hands from the wrists.

9)   PUSHING - To thrust either one or both arms away from the body in any direction.

10)   PULLING - To draw either one or both arms inwards from any direction.

11)   ARM SWINGS - A pendulum movement of either one or both arms in any direction.

HAND POSITIONS & MOVEMENTS

1) Fingers extended and apart with the palms facing any direction i.e. fanned.
2) Fingers and thumbs closed together.
3) Clap i.e. to strike the palms of the hands together.
4) Hands relaxed as for shaking.
5) Fingers together stretched upwards and the thumb stretched downwards. i.e. "dove" hand.
6) Fist clenched.
7) Pointing. (normally done with the index finger).
8) Snap i.e. a "click" using a finger against a thumb.
9) Hand Rolls i.e. A circular movement of both hands around each other either forwards or backwards.

ASSOCIATE

BODY MOVEMENTS

CONTRACTION - An inward pull of muscle tension. When a muscle contracts it shortens, hardens and broadens.

RELAXATION - The release of all tension from the body allowing the limbs to become limp and heavy.

MIDDLE BODY MOVEMENT - The expansion and contraction of the diaphragm. This can be used as an isolated action or in conjunction with pelvic action.

RIB CAGE MOVEMENT - The isolated movement of the rib cage in any direction.

SHOULDER MOVEMENT - The isolated movement of either one or both shoulders in any direction. The fast alternating movement of both shoulders is also known as to 'Shimmy'.

BODY BENDING - To curve the body either forwards, backwards or laterally. A combination of these can be used.

SWAY - To incline the body to right or left.

BOUNCE - A light up and down movement brought about by the flexing and straightening of the knees and ankles. (There was a lot more bounce action used in the earlier days of Disco/Freestyle particularly in the younger age groups but this has generally been replaced with more "earthy" movements.)

SHAKE - To use rapid vibrating movements.

BODY STRETCHING - To extend and expand one or more parts of the body either singularly or collectively.

RHYTHMICAL BODY ACTION - This describes movements that enable the dancer to express the rhythm of the music and is sometimes referred to as "body reaction".

EXPANSION - To extend one or more parts of the body thereby to increase in length and/or width and height.

CIRCULAR ACTION - The continuous rotational movement of any part of the body, e.g., wrists, hips, ankles.

PELVIC ACTION -The forward and/or backward tilt of the pelvis. This can be performed whilst the weight is central or when moving from foot to foot in co-ordination with foot and leg actions whilst transferring weight. These movements are best performed with the knees flexed.

HIP ACTION - A movement of the hips in any direction e.g., forwards, backwards, to side, circular.

MERENGUE ACTION - A hip movement in opposition to the stepping foot i.e. A step is taken without weight transfer and with a delayed hip action. As the next step is taken weight is then transferred onto the foot that was moved first and the hip is moved across.

FOOT & LEG ACTION - The use of the toe, ankle and knee joints to collect, control and transfer body weight and so produce the character of the dance form e.g. when running, jumping, springing etc.

RIPPLE - A wave like movement that travels from one part of the body through a series of interconnected body parts.

UPWARD BODY RIPPLE - The pelvis is tilted backwards and the knees flexed. The diaphragm and rib cage is then expanded and the pelvis tilted forward allowing the body to contract. The knees are then straightened and the diaphragm and rib cage are expanded. The head is then raised to complete the ripple.
DOWNWARD BODY RIPPLE - A complete reversal of the "Upward Body Ripple".

FORWARD ROLL* - This can be a dangerous movement if not taught correctly. It can be commenced in squatting position with hands on floor and head well tucked into the chest. The body is then rolled forwards to enable the shoulders to make contact with the floor. The roll is then continued to finish in sitting, standing or splits position.

HAND HOLDS USED IN COUPLES WORK

Hand holds are more often used in Boy/Girl couples work than in "All Girls" routines. When facing partner any combination of single hand holds can be used i.e. Right + Left, Left + Right, Left + Left or Right + Right . ("Hand shake hold").
Double hand holds can either be a straight forward Left/Right + Right/Left or arms crossed to achieve a Right/Right + Left /Left combination.
Side by side choreography sometimes requires a hand hold and is either Right + Left or Left +Right.
In "shadow" position hand holds can either be single i.e. Left + Left or Right + Right or double i.e. Left/Left plus Right/Right. From any of these hand holds the partner in front can make half a turn to end facing the other partner.

CONTEMPORARY ARM AND HAND MOVEMENTS

These are movements, shapes or positions that are currently in vogue and may change with new trends. As Freestyle is still a constantly developing form of dance there are many new arm and hand movements that are commonly used. Teachers taking their professional examinations should be aware of these and be able to describe and demonstrate several different examples.

FELLOWSHIP

JAZZ-LINE - To stand with feet apart and one knee slightly inverted.

CONTRA BODY MOVEMENT (CBM) - The turning of the opposite side of the body towards the stepping foot. This is usually used to assist turn.

CONTRA BODY MOVEMENT POSITION (CBMP) - The placing of the stepping foot across the path of the standing foot. This is usually used for effect, e.g., when dancing a Check.

HUG HOLD - The wrapping of both arms across and around the front of the body.

FLOORWORK - This term is used to collectively describe movements performed with at least part of the body in contact with the floor, e.g., splits, forward roll, cat stretch, etc.

FOOT POSITIONS -
1.   Heels together and toes turned out
2.   Feet apart with toes turned out
3.   Heel of right foot closed to instep of left foot.
4.   Both feet closed together and parallel.

—-ooo000ooo—-

SAMPLE QUESTIONS FOR ALL GRADES
A greater depth of questioning can be expected at Fellowship level to establish a deeper understanding of all the Body, Head, Arm and Hand movements.

A few examples of the type of questions that one should be prepared for are as follows:-
1)   How does the contraction and relaxation of muscles affect the movements that we perform?
2)   Are there any particular precautions that we should be aware of when using isolated movements of certain parts of the body?
3-5) Give at least 2 examples of how the middle body, rib cage and shoulder movements can be used within a routine to include different timings?
6)   Body stretching is defined in this section. How is the stretching of various muscles relevant to dance?
7)   Contemporary arm/hand movements - several examples for Licentiate and Fellowship grades.
8)   Demonstrate the merengue action giving 2 different timings and arm/hand movements.

ASSOCIATE
GENERAL
SAFETY
CLASSWORK
SOLO ROUTINE

LICENTIATE
PAIRS ROUTINE
TEAM ROUTINE

FELLOWSHIP
QUESTIONS
TEMPO
SLOW DANCE
STREET DANCE
CHOREOGRAPHY

TEACHING ABILITY

ASSOCIATE

GENERAL

This is possibly the most important section of a professional examination because it gives a good indication as to whether the teacher has the right "ingredients".

Teaching ability can be assessed on many qualities to include:- the presentation of work (this could involve a breakdown of the teachers demonstration routines in order to ascertain how they would be taught to a class), knowledge of faults i.e. their causes and methods of correction plus general teaching methods for all ages and grades. It is important that all answers are given in a confident manner with good voice projection and clarity of explanation.

This section can be difficult to prepare for, as there are no laid down questions. However, a well experienced teacher is unlikely to have problems with this section of the examination as they need only call upon their own experiences and methods of teaching to answer the questions

Methods of teaching that work for some schools in one part of the country might have a totally different response somewhere else. Likewise, ideas that teachers find successful with young children can work for some, and others might find that a different approach works better for them. etc..

Personality and projection are important qualities in a dance teacher. It is not always the acquiring of knowledge that is the most difficult but the imparting of it to other people in an easy and enjoyable manner.

There are many points that need to be covered in this section appertaining to some of the basic principles of Freestyle Dance and I hope that some of the points raised will "trigger -off" food for thought particularly in those preparing to take a professional examination.

SAFETY

There has always been a lot of concern relating to the safety aspect of Freestyle Dance and rightly so.

It is very important that only fully qualified teachers of dance conduct classes and/or lessons in this dance form and that they realise all the implications that can arise through injury to pupils. Hence, one of the reasons for the understanding of Basic Anatomy within the professional training for Freestyle qualifications.

The type of floor surface is most important and as with aerobics and fitness classes it is much safer and kinder on bones and joints if this type of dancing can be performed on a sprung floor. Solid floors should indicate to the teacher that certain steps and movements would be better avoided e.g. leaps, jumps and acrobatic work.

Teachers have a responsibility to their pupils and should not take any risks whatsoever - "if in doubt, leave it out!"

Footwear is also very important to prevent damage to foot and knee joints. Freestyle dancing is still similar to Contemporary dance in the fact that bare feet is usually the normal for performing. However, during practise it is advisable for dancers beyond beginner grade to wear some suitable footwear. Beginners are more likely to be performing simple movements with little degree of spring or bounce and are therefore less affected but could well benefit by wearing simple pumps or trainers to avoid splinters and keep their feet warm and hence more flexible. Jazz shoes are normally worn by higher grade dancers and more recently the "step" type of training shoe has been used a lot as it affords extra protection to the foot, particularly when many hours of work are to be done.

Always make sure that the class is well structured and has a warm-up section at the beginning and a cool down at the end. Be aware of the age and ability of the pupils in each class and make sure that the programme is tailored to their capabilities.

Never allow a pupil to dance with an injury. They are much better advised to sit it out so as not to prolong or impair their recovery.

Make sure that there is the right proportion of warmth and ventilation in the room and that everyone has enough space to be able to dance properly. If necessary, split the class into "heats". This can give one half the chance to catch their breath while the remainder take their turn. Obviously the change over between groups needs to be fairly quick particularly in the winter to avoid them cooling down before the end of class.
Another good rule is to ban "chewing" whilst dancing. This can be highly dangerous as it could lead to choking or asphyxia.

Many of these points are common sense but worth a quick reminder particularly when teachers are often so busy conducting the classes, sorting out problems and answering the phone etc. that sometimes the obvious passes us by.
It is of utmost importance that our pupils be taught correctly so as not to tempt injury of any kind. This applies also to the most basic of movements which must be taught with correct posture and technique. To reiterate on the question of difficult or controversial movements, they are best left to the most high grade dancers and only then under the strictest of supervision and control. Contra-indicated movements include full circular head rolls, knee drops, knee spins and any actions that place undue strain on the joints of the body.

CLASS WORK
Solo work is the subject that candidates at this level must be prepared for. However it must be remembered that the whole concept of **class work** is a very important part of Freestyle Dance and one should be conversant with this subject at all levels.

The methods that teachers use for beginners of all ages are very important because these obviously constitute the future of the school. Questions to consider:-

1)   How do you help very young beginners to hear the beat of the music and then start them to dance on the correct count?

2)   What type of routines would you use for young beginners? i.e.. Length of routine? Changes of direction? Speed of music? etc.

3)   What is your first approach to a new class of
                  a) very young beginners?
                  b) teenage beginners?
                  c) middle-aged beginners?

4)   At what speed do you teach brand new routines? Does this alter for different age groups or grades and if so, why?

Children and adults with special needs must also be considered in classes for all ages. Obviously a different approach would be needed for each person's particular situation. The main aim - to include the person as much as possible within the class without changing the general format and direction for the rest of the pupils. To move onto the concept of solo Freestyle work it would be quite useful to consider a "linking" question of some sort. e.g. How do you start to bring about the transition from class routines to solo work? The answers to this question will obviously vary considerably depending on the type of work that the teacher uses within their class.

SOLO ROUTINE

To develop a good solo routine there are several basic principles that will help to create good style and technique:-

1)   Good timing is of course essential as with any other form of dance. If there are certain steps or movements that tend to take a dancer "off time" it is best to avoid them. (This is more likely to be the case with beginners and starter pupils).

2)   The choreography of the routines needs to be tailored to the age, grade and capabilities of the dancer. Ideally it is best to try and bring out of each individual the style that will suit them in order to show them off to the best of their ability. Not all pupils will be as good at the same steps and movements as others in their grade and therefore it is better not to stereotype each dancer but to bring out the best in all by trying work to suit the individual. Steps and movements should naturally "flow" from one group to the next. A better result will be achieved if the dancer is not "wrong footed" through having to try and use the same foot twice without having enough time in the music to correct their balance.

3)   Extension and projection are important aspects of Freestyle dance. The same routine could be given to several different dancers but the success of the individual will very much depend on the degree of projection and extension that the pupil is able to express.

To assist the dancer with these qualities, the teacher can ensure that there is a good proportion of travelling (locomotive) and stationary (non-locomotive) actions within the routine. There also needs to be enough of the type of steps and movements included that make it easy for the dancer to project e.g.. runs, leaps, spins, kicks etc.,. and a lesser number of movements that make projection and extension harder e.g. floorwork.

Floorwork is an integral part of Freestyle dance but is not essential. Floorwork in moderation is probably a good yardstick but is best suited to the more supple and flexible dancers.

Another way of helping to produce projection and extension is to develop routines that have a general direction so that the dancer has the feel of progression around the room interspersed with variations and actions that create individuality.

4)   Presentation is all important as with all forms of dance. From the way in which the dancer is dressed and groomed to the way that they perform their work. It is up to the teacher to advise and coach in all these matters so as to achieve the best results from all their work. Remember that dance is an art form and therefore needs to be aesthetic to the human eye in every detail possible.

5)   Personality is an attribute that in most cases either does or does not come naturally to the individual dancer.

However, it is possible for the teacher to assist in this matter by explaining the importance of facial expression and giving the pupil ideas that could be tried throughout the routine. Building confidence is a great help towards improving floor personality and any way that this can be developed should be employed.

6)   Freestyle dance contains a great variety of steps and movements particularly in the higher grade dancers that continue to develop and diversify. However, if one was asked to name the 3 "basic ingredients" of Freestyle dance relating to solo work it would most certainly include runs, spins and kicks. Almost all dancers in intermediate grades and above will perform these steps in their routine in one form or another.

Beginners generally use less progressive types of movements but will normally have a few running steps in their routines

Kicks are often introduced at starter level and spins developed for Intermediate and above.

Due to the wide usage of these basic steps it is worth giving some attention to the ways in which we should develop them:-

RUNS:- Forward runs are best performed with the weight held over the balls of the feet, the rib cage and head uplifted, the toes turned outwards and the arms used in opposition to the legs.

"Drag runs" are better to be avoided. Some schools encourage this type of action on *all* forward runs and this can lead to the gradual development of poor technique and sometimes injury. Rather than producing a good turnout of the feet, the reverse starts to develop so that the feet gradually turn more and more inwards until the dancer can end up looking very "pigeon toed". Through constantly dragging the underside of the toes along the floor, the toe nails can start to split and become permanently damaged. This teaching method is not good and should be discouraged as dancers who have been taught to do this often find it difficult to re-adjust.

Backwards runs look better when a series of small steps are used rather than big strides. The weight should be well forward and the arm movements can be varied but are not so attractive when opposition arms are used.

KICKS:- Kicks need to ultimately aim high so that the dancer, on reaching the higher grades has the full range that they can use e.g. high kicks, flicks, hitch kicks etc.

It is a good idea to introduce little workout routines within the classes that will develop kicks. Obviously these need to be rehearsed after the dancer has warmed up so that there is no fear of hamstring injury.

Kicks with the toe pointed downwards should be developed to start with so that good technique is established. Karate-type kicks are sometimes used, particularly by the male solo dancers but a nice pointed toe is very attractive to the eye particularly in younger children.

A good kick should have height, a pointed toe and a straight leg. These qualities are best developed in the younger children and then they can be diversified at a later stage if desired.

SPINS:- These can be performed as a non-locomotive action or used for travel i.e. progressive spins.

Progressive spins must be developed to travel in a straight line. Most dancers have a preference as to whether they spin to the right or the left whilst some are able to spin equally well in both directions. If they have a preference it is best to establish which direction suits them the best in order to make the pupil feel more comfortable with the movement and hence achieve a top quality performance.

Spotting" needs to be developed in order that the dancer learns to spin in the correct manner. To achieve this, the head must be held high with eyes always concentrating on the direction of travel and the body poised correctly with the weight over the balls of the feet. Arm positions can be varied as the dancer gains confidence with the spins (See also "Spotting" in Definitions).

LICENTIATE

The subjects that require special attention at this level are Pairs and Team work.

PAIRS ROUTINE (DOUBLES/COUPLES)

After deliberating on the important qualities required to produce the best from a dancer in a solo performance we need to focus on the additional aspects that need specific attention when choreographing a couples routine:-

1)   The movements and steps that are used in the routine must be within the grasp of <u>both</u> dancers.

It is not advisable to use steps at which the one dancer excels but the other partner is much weaker as this will only highlight the weakness of the one instead of improving the overall ability of the couple.

Use movements that both can perform with ease and are suitable for the age and grade of the couple.

2)   Matching of the movements are important particularly in same sex couples which require a great deal of co-ordination. For this reason it is an easier task if the pair are of similar height and build. If one is significantly taller than the other it is best not to have this one in front of their partner at any stage throughout the routine.

3)   Variation of positions adds interest to a pairs routine and should be developed particularly in the higher grades:- Side by side, one in front of the other, shadow position and one partner facing the other all work well in combination. "Back to back" is not a good idea as it is hard to stay well matched. Different hand holds, body lines and arm positions all help to add variety and interest.

4)   Boy/Girl couples are a totally different concept to same sex couples and should be approached with contrast in mind. They should have work which allows the boy to take the lead and therefore move his partner in and out of varied steps and movements.

A lot of thought needs to be given to the type of steps that would be used for Boy/Girl couples as opposed to same sex couples and vice versa.

TEAM ROUTINE

Team work is an important way of disciplining dancers and provides a good nucleus for any dance school. It gives children of all ages and grades the experience of working closely with other dancers and the chance to develop team-spirit.

As with solo and pairs work it is also important that the team choreography is suitable for the age and capabilities of the dancers involved.

Beginners teams need to be kept simple. It is usually best to keep to one record with an easy beat, not many pattern changes and plenty of basic steps and movements that are effective but not intricate.It is very important to work for straight lines and positive patterns and that is why the work involved must be suitable for the dancers involved.

Try not to have the taller dancers at the front of the team even if they are the better movers. Higher grade teams should involve plenty of pattern changes and good use of music. i.e.. the interpretation of as many interesting phrases as possible.

Smart outfits, over-all good presentation and a very well rehearsed team add to a polished "end result".

FELLOWSHIP

Teaching ability is the section that can provide the most scope for ascertaining the experience of a teacher.

As well as experience in the training of solos, pairs and teams, the training of professionals will obviously be most important, as with any other branch it is the most important aspect for the future of the dance form.

The experience of the teacher to develop dancers from one level to another is also important and a selection of questions to include the aspect of training professionals will perhaps give some more "food for thought":-

1) Discuss and/or demonstrate ways in which the medal routine in the Demonstration section could be developed into a Starter or Intermediate solo routine?

2) Which steps or movements could be most easily added to the routine in order to bring it up to the level of a higher grade dance?

3) When training a professional candidate what are the most important aspects of the technique that need to be brought to the forefront and why?

4) When preparing a candidate for a professional examination do you think it is important for them to have an understanding of other forms of dance and if so, which aspects have been used for their training methods?

5) What do you consider to be the most important aspect when training a professional candidate for a Freestyle examination in comparison to any other dance forms that you may have taught?

6) Do you believe that Freestyle is a dance form for all ages and if so how do you develop classes that cater for the more mature person?

7) What individual requirements do you consider important when teaching children or adults with disabilities or special needs?

8) What aspects of Freestyle would you like to see developed and which aspects in your opinion do you see which detract from it's development?

More "food for thought":-

9) How do you see the future of dance in this country?

10) Do you consider dance to be a major growth industry? If so what methods would you like to see employed for this to continue and if not what ideas do you have to bring this about?

TEMPO

At Fellowship level it is also important to understand a little more about the TEMPO of the music rather than just its definition.

A teacher should be familiar with the specific tempi of "slow", "medium", "fast" and "very fast" music that they use when teaching. e.g., in 4/4 timing:-

SLOW = approx. 60-80 beats per minute (15-20 bars per minute).

MEDIUM = approx. 80-100 beats per minute (20-25 bars per minute).

FAST = approx. 100-120 beats per minute (25-30 bars per minute).

VERY FAST = anything above 120 beats per minute (30 bars per minute).

It is important to teach Freestyle work slowly to start with in order to develop good timing, correct poise and sound technique.

For mature dancers it is always best to keep to a steady beat so that they can enjoy the work and feel well exercised at the end of a class but not totally exhausted!

SLOW DANCE

The first Slow Dance competition was introduced to the UK by David & Anna Jones at the Dancer of the Year Championships in 1993. Slow Dance competitions are now popular at many Freestyle events throughout the country and this is an excellent trend because it gives the dancers chance to express themselves at different tempi.

The type of work used further bridges the gap between the Theatre and the Ballroom branches. Slow music is used at a tempo of approximately 60-80 beats per minute (15 - 20 bars per minute). At this speed all of the movements can be developed further than during fast dance in order to produce good body shapes and lines.

A good variety of movements should be included within the choreography to produce a stylish and well-presented performance.

A Slow Dance routine should not be the same as that used for fast dance because some of the movements do not suit the slow music. It can look like a slow-motion routine rather than a piece of work specifically designed for Slow Dance. Types of steps and/or movements to avoid include runs, cross-tap kicks, switch turns and kick/flick ball changes.

This form of Freestyle has enormous potential and benefits. It provides an experience of balletic work and encourages the dancer to clearly define their actions showing good balance and co-ordination.

Foot pressure into the floor through the balls of the feet is particularly important in order to produce strength through the ankles. It is also important to encourage good toning of the feet, particularly in Slow Dance work. Emphasis is also placed on good presentation and projection, and therefore this form of dance should be encouraged within the Freestyle curriculum.

STREET DANCE

Street Dance or "Hip-Hop" as it is also named is a form of dance that has influenced and integrated with Freestyle over recent years.

It incorporates "Body Popping" and " Break Dancing" and is widely used by "backing dancers" on pop videos.

The tempo used is approximately 80-100 beats per minute (20-25 bars per minute) and is therefore of an intermediate speed between Slow Dance and fast Freestyle.

This form of dance has also become popular at many Freestyle competitions where events for all age groups are often held. Street Dance can also be defined in the same way as Freestyle Dance (see page 13). However, there is in Street Dance a great emphasis placed on syncopated timing plus the use of "slow" counts in order to create the effect of "light and shade" (see under "Choreography").

Routines in Street Dance can be choreographed to a specific track and the actions are used to interpret the lyrics of the song. These actions can be strong and vibrant or very subtle. Many of the basic steps and movements within *Freestyle Dance* can be interpreted in Street Dance mode.

This dance form also has enormous potential and allows the individual dancer freedom to express themselves to the music. Casual clothing is normally worn for this type of dance with sports shoes ("trainers") as footwear.

CHOREOGRAPHY

Choreography is an integral part of Freestyle Dance. The most important point to remember is that the choreography must suit the age and ability of the dancers that are being trained.

It is much better that the individual dancers are at ease with the work whether it be classwork or competition routines. Nobody usually likes to feel "out of their depth" and therefore it is better to start off with steady, easy to follow work and then to "build on basics".

Foot positions are the first stage, followed by the body actions and then arm and hand movements. Obviously, different teachers all have different methods and whatever produces the best results must be the right formula.

Young people in particular normally respond best to music that they can identify with and therefore better success is usually achieved by using "up to date" music. This usually gives more inspiration to the teacher when choreographing a routine and therefore works better all round than "blowing the dust" off a well worn record when producing a new routine.

Beginners work is best kept to one step or movement per beat so that they adopt a very definite understanding of dancing on time to the music..

As dancers progress it is then possible to "play" with the beats in a bar.
The most common methods are to:-
1)   Take 2 beats to perform a step or movement instead of 1 beat, thus producing a count of "slow".
2)   Split 2 beats into 3 parts i.e. instead of counting 12, the count will become 1 & 2, thus producing a count of "quick" and "quick". (See 'Timing' on page 16.)

By playing with the timing in this way we can produce a greater variety of steps and movements with different interpretations therefore creating "light and shade" within the choreography.

Experimentation is the best way to develop new work - "Nothing ventured - nothing gained". Continued experience helps to develop the knowledge of the types of ideas that work well and those that do not "gel" so easily,

Each movement must "flow" into the next step so that the routine is fluent. It must not "jump" from one move to another and should be as easy to dance as possible.

Trial and error is the name of the game as long as the work is kept safe and easy to follow. A successful routine is one that looks easy to dance, is aesthetic to the eye and is enjoyable for the performer.
The final section of the book includes routines of varying grades which I hope will be of use either as classwork, medal work, ideas for the training of competitors and/or for use in professional examinations.

SECTION 8 - FREESTYLE ROUTINES

INTRODUCTION

The following three routines are suggested for use in class work suitable at beginner, intermediate and advance levels. They can also be used in the choreography of solos, pairs and trios and provide some ideas for team work.

The routines can also provide ideas for the demonstration section of the professional examination. They can be sub-divided into shorter routines or extended to create more comprehensive routines.

They have been given headings of Beginner, Intermediate and Advanced as a rough guide. Teachers may grade them differently according to the type of work used at their school.

It is always best to teach new routines slowly and to count before trying them to a steady beat, then gradually increasing the tempo. This is the best way to develop good technique and achieve the precision on each movement that is required to produce an ultimately good performance.

ABBREVIATIONS

R	=	Right
L	=	Left
F	=	Foot
RF	=	Right Foot
LF	=	Left Foot
H	=	Heel
T	=	Toe
BOF	=	Ball (s) of foot (feet)
LOD	=	Line of Dance
w/o	=	Without weight.

TWISTY ARMS

BAR	STEPS AND MOVEMENTS	COUNT
1.	Four fwd runs RF,LF,RF,LF, leading with opp arms to legs.	1234
2.	Step RF to side making ¼ turn to L with knees slightly flexed. (Arms stretched fwds in parallel Position, palms downwards and fists clenched).	1
	Close LF to RF with knees straight. (Turn arms inwards, palms upwards and fist clenched).	2
	Repeat previous 12	34
3.	Three little jumps with feet together and knees slightly flexed making ½ turn to R. (Arms stretched fwds in parallel Pos, palms upwards and fists clenched).	1&2
	Bend fwd and touch floor.	3
	Stand up straight.	4
4.	Step LF across in front of RF. (Cross arms around body).	1
	Step RF to side large step (R arm Diag high. L arm Diag low).	2
	Repeat previous 12.	34
5.	Close LF to RF and flex both knees.	1
	Jump with feet together to make ¾ turn to R, ending with feet apart and knees flexed.	2
	Bend fwd and touch the floor.	3
	Stand up straight.	4
6.	Feet still apart knees flexed. (Clench R fist and tap twice onto L knee).	12
	Pos held. (Clench L fist and tap twice on R knee).	34
7.	Straighten knees. (Clap hands twice above head).	12
	Pos held. (Roll arms around each other in front of body then extend both arms fwd in parallel Pos with fingers pointed).	34
8.	Rotate hips twice in clockwise direction. (Arms stretched fwds with hands clasped).	1234
9.	Rotate hips twice in anti-clockwise direction. (Arms stretched fwds with hands clasped).	1234
10.	Four walks bwds, RF, LF, RF, LF. (Bring arms inwards towards body then extend them slowly fwds).	1234
11.	Little runs bwds with body inclined fwds and knees slightly flexed. (Arms stretched fwds).	1&2&3&4

RUNS INTO A SWITCH

BAR	*STEPS AND MOVEMENTS*	*COUNT*
1.	Four fwd runs starting with the RF.	1234
2.	Switch turn leading with RF making ½ turn to L.	12
	Repeat previous 12.	34
3.	Chasse to R with knees compressed. (Click both hands in front of body).	1&2
	Spring low into knees. (Punch both arms fwds three times).	3&4
4.	Whisk turn crossing LF behind RF making a complete turn to R.	
	(Circle both arms upwards and outwards).	12
	Step RF to side and touch floor.	3
	Stand up straight.	4
5.	Cross RF in front of LF. (Cross arms in front of body).	1
	Point LF to side. (Extend both arms upwards and touch back of wrists together).`	2
	Cross LF in front of RF. (Bring arms down to horizontal pos).	3
	Kick R leg upwards with T pointed. (Arm position held).	4
6.	Cross RF in front of LF.	1
	Lift LF, make a complete turn to L and place LF to side.	2
	Flex knees and tap both fists onto knees three times.	3&4
7.	Cross RF in front of LF and straighten knees. (Extend both arms upwards into high V).	1
	Step LF to side and lower into knees. (Bring arms down into Low V).	2
	Repeat previous 12.	34
8.	With knees slightly flexed (Hands clasped, tap hands onto R knee then L knee and then extend both arms across to L side of body).	1&2
	Step RF across in front of LF.	3
	Replace weight onto Ball of LF.	&
	Step RF to side.	4
9.	Slow hip roll. (Arms down at sides).	12
	Faster hip rolls. (Extend arms upwards).	3&4
10.	Take little runs backwards bringing feet close together.	
	(Extend both arms fwds).	1&2&3&4
11.	Spring feet apart. (Arms into High V).	1
	Close feet together. (Bring hands in towards middle body).	2
	Chasse to R. (R arm Diag high and L arm low, then L arm Diag high and R arm low and then reverse again).	3&4
12.	Step LF slightly across RF. (Arms into High V).	1
	Kick R leg upwards with Toe pointed. (Bring arms down to horizontal Pos).	2
	Cross RF in front of LF.	3
	Making a complete turn to the L tap RF to side of LF. (Raise R arm to shoulder height and click fingers).	4

13. Open turn RLR making a complete turn to R. 1&2
Close LF to RF and move hips from side to side RLR. (Arms down at sides). 3&4

14. Lower into knees slightly. 1
Spring upwards making a complete turn to R landing with feet apart and knees flexed. 2
Feet pos held. (Circle both arms outwards from the elbows). 3&
Straighten L leg and turn R knee inwards to create "Jazz line."
(Extend both arms across to L side of body with palms of hands upwards). 4

15. Cross RF in front of LF. (Bring both hands in front of body to cross each other). 1
Flick L leg backwards. (Raise R arm high and take L arm out to side). 2
Cross LF in front of RF. (Lower arms to horizontal pos). 3
Pivot on LF making a complete turn to R landing with RF to side and knees flexed. 4

16. Three walks bwds LRL. (Arms down at sides with palms facing forwards). 123
Ball change RL. (Rotate arms at sides, waist level). &4

ADVANCED
BODY REACTION

BAR	*STEPS AND MOVEMENTS*	*COUNT*
1.	Four fwd walks commencing on RF	1234
2.	Step RF fwd and rondé LF close to floor making a complete turn to R	12
	Stand with feet apart (Arms in High V)	3
	Create jazz line by flexing and inverting R knee slightly	4
3.	Check RF fwd and across, replace wt onto LF and return RF to original position.	1&2
	Step RF to side flex both knees making ¼ turn to L (R arm extended to R side)	34
4.	Step RF to side with legs straight making ¼ turn to R (Extend both arms to R)	1
	Position held (Extend both arm to L)	2
	Position held (Rotate both arms at elbows)	3&
	Position held (Extend both arms fwd into parallel position)	4
5.	Cross - tap - kick commencing on RF	1234
6.	Cross turn commencing on RF making a complete turn to L	12
	Point RF to side w/o wt (Extend R arm to side and click fingers)	3
	Cross RF behind LF w/o wt (Cross R arm in front of body and click fingers)	4
7.	Whisk Turn on RF making a complete turn to R	12
	Step RF to side turning head to R (Extend both arms to R above head)	3
	Position held, turn head to L (Extend both arms to L above head)	4
8.	Step RF fwd and across LF turning ¼ to L	1
	Step LF fwd and across RF turning ¼ to R	2
	Flick RF fwd	3
	Swivel on ball of LF making ½ turn to R	4
9.	Progressive spins to R commencing on RF	1&2&
	Two walks fwd RF, LF with alternate shoulder lifts	3&4
10.	Turn ½ to L on balls of feet allowing LF to cross in front of RF with flexing of the knees	12
	Position held (use body reaction)	34
11.	Progressive spins fwd commencing on either foot	1&2&3&4
12.	"Freeze" into a pose using contemporary hands and arms	1234
13.	Cross - tap - kick commencing on RF	1234
14.	Cross turn on RF making 7/8 turn to RF	12
	Extend RF fwd and flex both knees	34
	(Clasp hands high above head and push arms fwds twice)	

15.	Step RF back - a long step (Extend R arm fwds and L arm back)	12
	Swivel to R on balls of feet making 7/8 turn to L allowing RF to cross in front of LF (Swing L arm across front of body and R arm behind body with fists clenched)	34
16.	Close feet together and flex into knees	1
	Star jump with arms in High V	2
	Step RF to side making $1/4$ turn to R, flex knees and use body reaction	3&4
17.	Progressive spins commencing on RF making $1 1/4$ turns to R	1&2&
	Switch turn commencing fwd on RF making $1/2$ turn to L with flexing of knees (Extend both arms fwd in parallel position)	34